The lion and the mouse

Retold by Beverley Randell
from an Aesop fable
Illustrated by Pat Reynolds

One day, a little mouse
jumped onto a sleeping lion.

The lion woke up.

"**Got** you!" he said.

"Eee-eee!" said the mouse.

"Please let me go!

Please let me go!

One day I may help you."

"Ha-ha-ha," laughed the lion. "A little mouse like you can't help a big lion like me!"

But he let the mouse go.

"Thank you," said the little mouse, and away she ran to her hole.

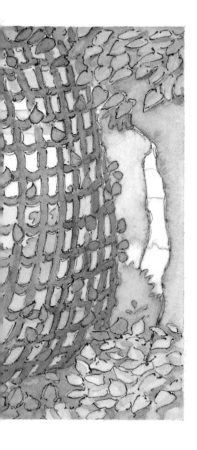

The lion laughed
at the little mouse.
He laughed
and laughed.
He did not see
the big net
by the trees,
and he walked into it.

"**Help**!" he roared.
"I can't get away!
Who will help me?
Who will come and help me?"

But no one came, all day.

Then, after the sun went down, the mouse came out of her hole. "The lion is roaring for help!" she said. "I'm coming!"

The mouse ran to help the lion. "I can make a hole in that net with my teeth," she said.

And she did. "You can get out now," said the mouse.

"**See**! A little mouse like me **did** help a big lion like you."

"Yes, I see," said the lion. "Yes, a mouse **can** help a lion. Thank you, little mouse."

"I am pleased I let you go,
little mouse," said the lion.
"So am I," said the mouse.